CROCODILES,
ALLIGATORS & LIZARDS

CROCODILES,
ALLIGATORS & LIZARDS

From Black Caimans to Komodo Dragons

DAVID ALDERTON

amber
BOOKS

Published by Amber Books Ltd
United House
North Road
London
N7 9DP
United Kingdom

www.amberbooks.co.uk
Instagram: amberbooksltd
Facebook: amberbooks
X (Twitter): @amberbooks
Pinterest: amberbooksltd

ISBN: 978-1-83886-428-6

Project Editor: Anna Brownbridge
Designer: Keren Harragan
Picture Research: Terry Forshaw

Printed in China

Contents

Introduction

Crocodilians and lizards reflect the huge diversity in size that exists within the world's 12,000 living species of reptile. The group also includes snakes, turtles and tortoises, plus the tuatara (*Sphenodon punctatus*). The biggest reptile of all is the giant saltwater crocodile (*Crocodylus porosus*), which can attain a length of more than 6m (19.7ft) and may reach a weight of about 1500kg (3300lb). At the other extreme, the Jaragua dwarf gecko (*Sphaerodactylus ariasae*)

is not just the smallest lizard but also the tiniest reptile. It typically grows up to no more than 14mm (0.55in) when adult and weighs just 0.13g (0.005 oz). Today's largest crocodilians would nevertheless have been dwarfed by the giants of the past. The biggest yet discovered, christened *Deinosuchus*, could attain a length of 11m (36ft) from nose to tail, and estimates suggest that it may have weighed as much as 3450kg (7610lb).

ABOVE:
Geckos like this leopard gecko (*Eublepharis macularius*) are generally able to climb well and are all relatively small lizards. The largest gecko – which became extinct in the 1800s – was *Gigarcanum delcourti*. It could reach a length of some 60cm (24in).

OPPOSITE:
Yacaré caimans (*Caiman yacare*) are seen here in Brazil's Pantanal region. Caimans rank amongst the smallest of crocodilians. This species typically grows to about 3m (9.8ft) in length. There are now 27 recognized species of living crocodilians, comprising crocodiles, alligators and caimans, and the gharials.

The Americas

This part of the world is home to 11 of the world's 27 living species of crocodilian. Those that can be encountered here include all members of the *Alligatoridae* family, which consists of both caimans and true alligators, apart from the Chinese alligator, which, as its name suggests, is found in Asia. There are only four crocodiles found in this region, however, and their range lies to the south of that of the American alligator, as they are less well-equipped to survive under cold conditions. The most northerly is the American crocodile (*Crocodylus acutus*), which is restricted to parts of Florida. This is the only region of the world where crocodiles and alligators live alongside each other, although this particular crocodile is also well-equipped to live in brackish and even saltwater, which has allowed it to colonize islands in the Caribbean.

There is a distinctive divide between lizards found in the Americas and those occurring elsewhere in the world. The large *Iguanidae* family, which consists of nearly 1000 species, is restricted almost entirely to the Americas. The ancestors of the only members of the family occurring elsewhere are thought to have drifted over 10,000km (6218 miles), ending up on the islands of Fiji and Tonga in the Pacific Ocean. Assuming this theory is correct, they have travelled further in this way to colonize a new area than any other vertebrate.

OPPOSITE:
Orinoco crocodile
An Orinoco crocodile (*Crocodylus intermedius*) hauling itself out of the water. They are characterized by their light colouration.

LEFT:
Cooling down
One of the ways that crocodilians can control their body temperature if they are getting too hot basking in the sun is by resting with their mouths open in this way. Such behaviour is described as 'mouth gaping'. Unlike us, crocodiles cannot sweat to cool down.

ABOVE TOP:
Hiding away
The eyes of crocodilians, like the Orinoco crocodile seen here, are located high up on the head, which helps these reptiles to conceal the rest of their bodies in the water while not compromising their ability to see around them. They are very stealthy predators.

ABOVE BOTTOM:
Hope for the future
The Orinoco crocodile is one of four species that are currently considered to be critically endangered. It is restricted to limited areas in Colombia and Venezuela. A captive-breeding programme has helped to boost the genetic diversity and numbers of the surviving wild population.

LEFT:

A different profile

The much broader snout of the American alligator (*Alligator mississippensis*) sets it apart from crocodiles. There is also a difference in dentition: the alligator's bottom teeth are concealed when the mouth is closed, whereas with crocodiles, the fourth tooth in the lower jaw is conspicuous.

ABOVE TOP:

Unusual foods?

Alligators look for their food, and this even includes seeking out a variety of fruit on land. They have been observed consuming citrus fruits, elderberries and grapes growing wild. In fact, these crocodilians may be significant in dispersing seeds through their range via their droppings.

ABOVE BOTTOM:

Getting a grip

The feet of American alligators are equipped with powerful claws, enabling them to climb up muddy banks relatively easily. There are five claws on each front foot and four on both of the hind feet. Webbing between the toes aids the swimming abilities of these reptiles.

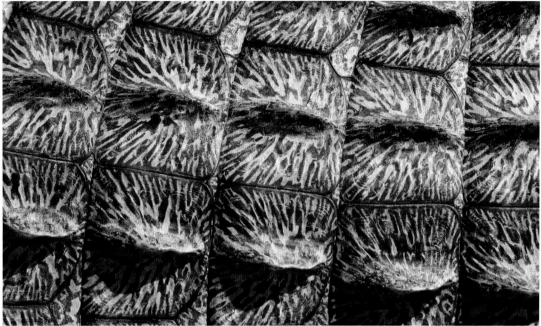

LEFT:
Maternal care
A young American alligator rests on its mother's back. Its orangish-yellow banding provides camouflage. At this stage, the hatchlings remain close to their mother, who watches over them. They communicate with her by their calls, venturing off to hunt invertebrates, amphibians and small fish.

ABOVE TOP:
Colour variants
The colour of an adult alligator's skin helps to distinguish it from that of a crocodile (seen here), with blackish scales along the back. Occasionally, albino alligators, recognizable by their white colouration, are seen, but being so conspicuous, they usually soon fall victim to predators.

ABOVE BOTTOM:
The start of life
An American alligator emerges from its egg. A clutch can comprise anywhere from 30–50 eggs, and the incubation period is about 65 days. The female will then carry her offspring carefully down to shallow water, scooping them up in her jaws to do so.

ABOVE TOP:
Size difference
Male American alligators, which are known as bulls, will grow significantly larger than females. They can reach over 4.6m (15ft), while a female is usually unlikely to get much bigger than 3m (9.8ft). Growth slows down considerably as alligators become older.

ABOVE BOTTOM:
Hunting abilities
American alligators can seize prey in shallow water. Their deadly strength comes from the bite force generated by snapping their jaws closed. Conversely, the muscles that open the mouth are surprisingly weak, so that an alligator's jaws can simply be held together safely by hand.

RIGHT:
No longer unchallenged
A typical American alligator habitat in the Florida Everglades is seen here. These reptiles are the apex predator in the region, although they have been joined by the Burmese python (*Python bivittatus*), an introduced species now living and breeding in the region that is known to prey on alligators.

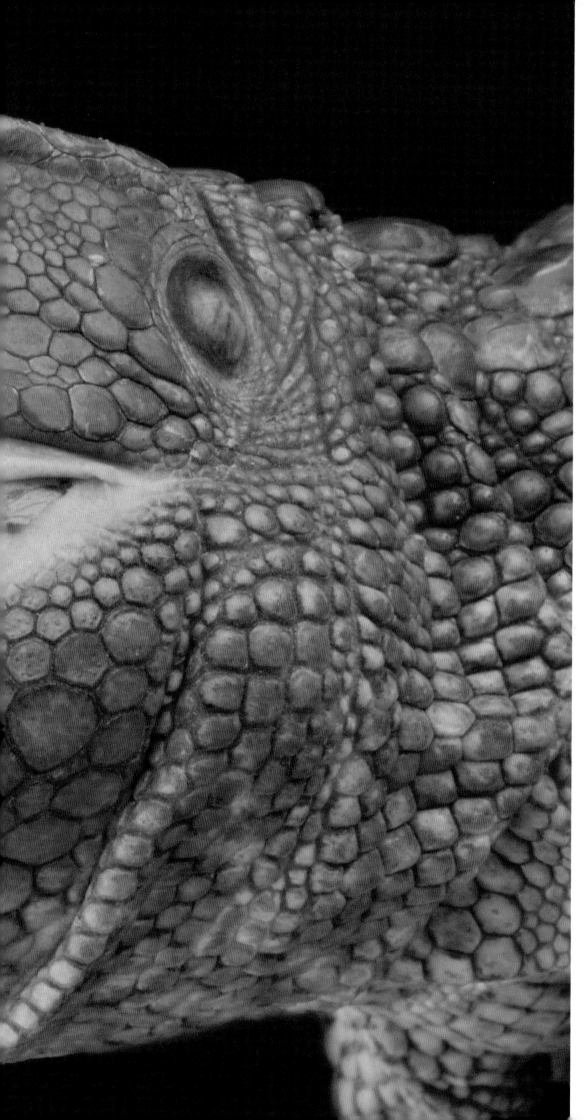

A crocodilian name
The northern caiman lizard
(*Dracaena guianensis*) occurs
in the northern part of South
America and is more brightly
coloured than its southern relative
(*D. paraguayensis*). Possessing
powerful teeth, these relatively
large lizards are close relatives of
the tegus. However, they are semi-
aquatic by nature.

Big head
Caiman lizards have a relatively large and broad head, which allows for the necessary musculature to enable them to crunch up their diet of hard-shelled invertebrates with relative ease.

At home in water
These lizards are quite at home in water, seeking food here and swimming well. They often rest on branches above water, dropping down to swim off and escape if disturbed.

Well-protected
The raised scales running down the back of caiman lizards have an appearance rather like those of a caiman and help to explain their common name, in conjunction with their tail and love of water.

OPPOSITE TOP:
Powerful limbs
The legs of caiman lizards are short yet powerful, with sharp claws at the end of each toe assisting the lizard's climbing abilities. The hind limbs provide the major thrust for swimming, with the third hind toe being significantly longer than the other three digits.

OPPOSITE BOTTOM:
Sight and size
Caiman lizards have special transparent eyelids that protect the eyes and yet allow them to see clearly when they are underwater. In terms of size, they rank as one of the largest South American lizards, growing up to about 1.2m (4ft) in length.

LEFT:
Unusual feeding habits
Aquatic snails feature prominently in the diet of caiman lizards, but they will also eat freshwater clams and crayfish. They dive down into the water to grab their prey and then rely on their powerful teeth to break through the shell, before spitting this out.

A Caribbean crocodilian
The Cuban crocodile (*Crocodylus rhombifer*) is a critically endangered species found only on the island of Cuba. It is not a particularly large crocodile, with the bigger males only growing up to 3.5m (11ft) in length. They can weigh 215kg (474lb).

Zapata Swamp
The distribution of the Cuban crocodile today has been reduced largely to the Zapata Swamp, although it also occurs on the Isla de la Juventud, which lies to the south of the main island. It has been heavily hunted – only about 4000 remain in the wild today.

LEFT:

Venturing onto land

The legs of the Cuban crocodile are strong, which enables it to move more easily on land than other crocodilians. In the past, there were totally terrestrial members of this group, some of which only went extinct less than 3000 years ago and so lived alongside people.

ABOVE TOP:

Working together

Cuban crocodiles can often be encountered in relatively shallow water, and it has been suggested that they may display cooperative hunting behaviour. They feed on fish and turtles as well as birds and mammals when the opportunity presents itself. This species may occasionally attack people.

ABOVE BOTTOM:

Water matters

Seen here swimming in a coastal mangrove swamp, Cuban crocodiles can also be encountered in river estuaries rather than just being confined to areas of freshwater. The Zapata swamp, which is their last surviving refuge, extends over an area of 4000 sq km (one million acres).

A dwarf form

Cuvier's dwarf caiman (*Paleosuchus palpebrosus*) is the smallest New World crocodilian, with females (who are not as large as males) averaging about 1.4 metres (4.6ft) long and weighing approximately 5kg (11lb). This caiman also ranks as the smallest of all living crocodilians.

LEFT:
Key features
The head of Cuvier's dwarf caiman is unusual among crocodilians, having a distinctly domed appearance and an upturned snout, with the upper jaw overhanging the lower. These South American caimans are nocturnal. They retreat to muddy burrows during hot weather if their pools dry up.

ABOVE TOP:
Early days
A young Cuvier's dwarf caiman reveals its small sharp teeth. As youngsters, these crocodilians feed mainly on invertebrates ranging from crabs to beetles, which may be caught either on land or in water. It may be eight years before hatchlings breed for the first time.

ABOVE BOTTOM:
Protection matters
Adult Cuvier's dwarf caimans are very well-protected by hard bony structures called osteoderms present under the skin. This is why they are not hunted for their skins to be made into leather (unlike most crocodilians). Females care for their young for about 20 months.

OPPOSITE:
A deadly nature
The Gila monster (*Heloderma suspectum*) is an unusual lizard, being one of the very few species that is venomous and can kill a person, although fatalities are very rare.

LEFT:
Hiding away
Much of the life of the Gila monster is spent underground in burrows. It occurs in the southwest of the United States, extending southwards down into the Mexican state of Sonora.

BELOW:
Eating well
Eggs of different types feature in the varied diet of the Gila monster. They will gorge themselves when food is available. Young can eat half their body weight in a single meal.

An unexpected benefit
Following scientific study, the
venom of the Gila monster
has actually proved to be
beneficial for people. One of
its components, exendin-4, was
found to be effective in regulating
cases of type 2 diabetes and is
now being synthesized artificially
for this purpose.

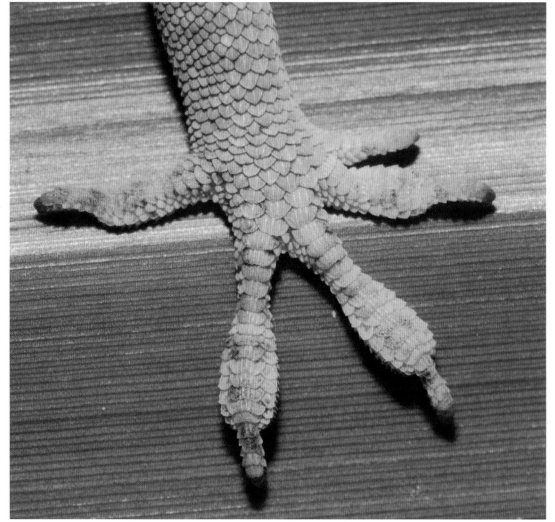

OPPOSITE:
Agile and adaptable
Weighing only somewhere between 3–7g (0.11–0.25 oz), the green anole (*Anolis carolinensis*) can climb very easily – not just on branches but also over flowers. They are capable of changing their colour to some extent, but not as effectively as true chameleons.

ABOVE:
An arboreal lifestyle
Most of the green anole's body length, which can be up to 20cm (8in) overall, consists of its tapering tail. These lizards live off the ground and hunt a wide variety of invertebrates. Females usually have a whitish strip along the back, as seen here.

LEFT:
Well-equipped to climb
The scales of the green anole, seen in this close-up on a front foot, extend right down over the toes, which terminate with small claws. The expanded area in the middle of each toe help these lizards to maintain their balance when they are climbing.

Communication
Green anoles communicate with each other by using this prominent pinkish-red flap of skin below their lower jaw known as a dewlap or throat fan. Males will inflate their dewlap to deter potential rivals, and it can also serve to attract females.

RIGHT TOP:

Keen eyesight

The vision of the green iguana (*Iguana iguana*) allows these lizards to see well in colour, and in fact, they can detect many more colours than us thanks to their ability to see into the ultraviolet spectrum. They can also detect movement in the distance.

RIGHT MIDDLE:

More variable

A green iguana's skin. Although described as green, their colouration can vary depending on their locality. Individuals from southerly parts of South America may display a decidedly bluish tinge to their bodies, and some Caribbean green iguanas are reddish, like those from western Costa Rica.

RIGHT BOTTOM:

Different shapes

While the scales on the body of a green iguana are relatively small and even in size, those on the head are much more variable in appearance. This prominent, roughly circular scale is called the subtympanic shield or plate and lies beneath the ear opening or tympanum.

OPPOSITE:

Lifestyle

In spite of their rather fearsome appearance, green iguanas are herbivores, feeding on plant matter, although youngsters feed more on invertebrates. They can climb well thanks to their powerful feet and will grip branches using just their hind toes to prevent or slow a fall.

OVERLEAF:

Size matters

Green iguanas may grow to 2m (6.6ft) long and weigh more than 9.1kg (20lb), ranking among the largest of the New World lizards. They are equipped to inflict a painful bite and use a long, whip-like tail to defend themselves.

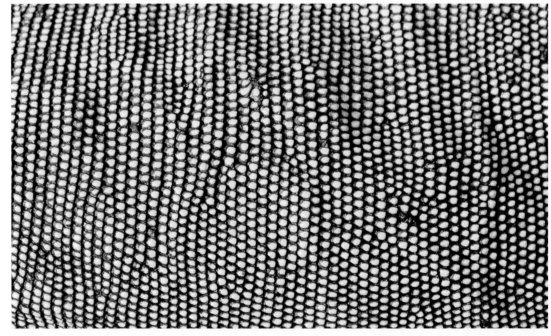

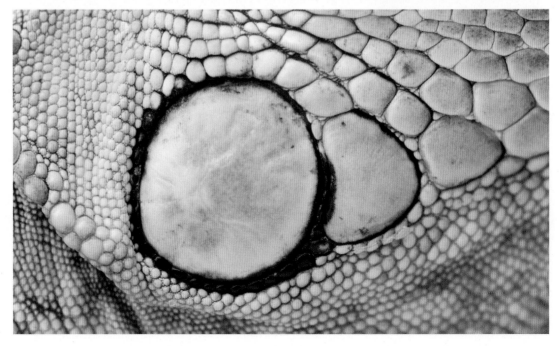

LEFT:
Growth and development
Morelet's crocodiles (*Crocodylus moreletii*) hatching. Incubation lasts about 80 days, with young hatchlings measuring about 17cm (6.5in). Adult males can subsequently grow to over 2.4m (8ft) – slightly larger than females. Breeding occurs at the start of the rainy season.

OVERLEAF LEFT TOP:
A silent killer
Like many crocodiles, the Morelet's is an opportunistic hunter, tracking its prey using stealth. They can launch themselves out of the water quickly to catch their quarry unawares on land. Large individuals will seize goats and even dogs in this way, and have attacked people.

OVERLEAF LEFT MIDDLE:
Tall scales
The tall scales running down the tail of a Morelet's crocodile can be seen when these reptiles surface. They may be damaged. One here shows what could be a tooth mark from an encounter with another crocodile, while the neighbouring scale is evidently broken.

OVERLEAF LEFT BOTTOM:
Identification
The colouration of Morelet's crocodile is a greyish-brown shade with blackish markings on the upper part of the body. It is generally darker overall than the American crocodile, which has a wider distribution in Central America. Morelet's young are bright yellow with dark banding.

Habitat

Morelet's is primarily a freshwater crocodile, inhabiting areas of Mexico, Belize and Guatemala, but occasionally it is seen in brackish water. It prefers secluded wooded areas or savannas, being at home in habits ranging from swampland to lakes and rivers. The young are shy and rarely observed.

ABOVE TOP:
Hiding in plain sight
The nostrils of crocodiles are raised above the overall level of the snout. This means that the reptile can continue breathing while remaining largely submerged and out of sight at the surface. The nostrils have flaps that are kept closed when the crocodile is underwater.

ABOVE BOTTOM:
Eyesight
In common with other crocodilians, Morelet's has a slit-shaped pupil, which adjusts to the prevailing amount of light. There is also a reflective layer, called the tapetum lucidum, which acts like a mirror, helping to reflect light back through the eye, improving nighttime vision.

RIGHT:
Lifestyle
A Morelet's crocodile is seen here in Mexico. The presence of the vegetation helps to conceal its presence while it sunbathes. When the crocodile submerges again, its external ear flaps will cover these auditory openings, keeping water out. These crocodiles also possess a keen sense of smell.

A semi-terrestrial crocodilian
Smooth-fronted caimans
(*Paleosuchus trigonatus*) live in
South America, in the Amazon
and Orinoco river basins. They
often spend time on land hiding in
the undergrowth, being described
as 'smooth-fronted' because they
lack the bony ridges (resembling
spectacles) of the spectacled
caiman (*Caiman crocodilus*).

Seen together
A group of caimans together, photographed in Brazil's Pantanal Swamp. During the dry season, these reptiles, although not especially social by nature, are effectively corralled into smaller areas. Their being more conspicuous at this stage means scientists can carry out accurate population surveys with drones.

LEFT:
Most widely-encountered
The spectacled caiman has the widest distribution of any caiman. This extends from southern Florida, where it has been introduced, down through Central America as far south as Peru, Brazil and possibly Bolivia. It can also be encountered on Caribbean islands, including Trinidad and Tobago.

BOTTOM LEFT:
Key characteristics
The eyes are well-protected by the eyelids, and in the case of the spectacled caiman, there is also a bony ridge resembling a pair of spectacles present at the top of the snout, just below the eyes. This accounts for the species's common name.

BOTTOM RIGHT:
Feeding habits
A spectacled caiman basks on a log. These small crocodilians will generally hunt at night. The larger males can overpower prey as large as wild pigs, but aquatic creatures, such as fish, crabs and snails, are more commonly consumed, often along with some plant matter.

Africa

A wide range of lizards as well as six types of crocodilian are to be found in Africa and on neighbouring offshore islands, such as Madagascar. This island has a particularly rich herpetofauna, although the native crocodile that used to be found there is now sadly extinct. It was a very distinctive type, known as a horned crocodile (*Voay robustus*), and even lived alongside people until about 1300 years ago. It is unclear as to why it disappeared – but climate change and/or hunting could have been responsible. Soon afterwards, Nile crocodiles from the mainland started to colonize Madagascar, and they remain resident on the island today.

Madagascar is also home to a number of endemic lizards, including chameleons. These species, occurring nowhere else on the planet, are particularly vulnerable to the effects of habitat change, especially given that they only occur in relatively small, localized areas on the island. Within mainland Africa itself, the very restricted ranges of some chameleons, for example, combined with the difficulty of accessing the areas where they live means that previously unknown species of lizard are still being discovered.

Recently, there has even been a new species of large crocodile found in Africa – the first of its kind in over 80 years. Now known as the Central African slender-snouted crocodile (*Mecistops leptorhynchus*), DNA studies have confirmed that it is a separate species from its close West African relative. Only an estimated 500 individuals of this previously unknown crocodilian are thought to survive.

OPPOSITE:
Bizarre and beautiful
One of Madagascar's spectacular chameleons. This is a panther chameleon (*Furcifer pardalis*), a species confined to eastern and northern parts of the island.

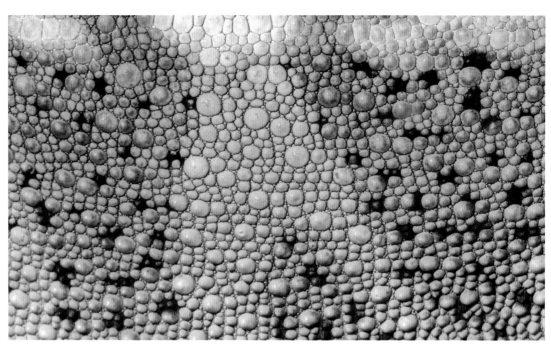

LEFT:
Poised to strike
A panther chameleon lines up to strike at potential prey, with its tongue starting to protrude from its mouth. Members of this group of lizards are able to swivel their eyes independently, which can help them to spot targets. They prey almost entirely on invertebrates.

ABOVE TOP:
Colour variations
The colourful appearance of chameleons can be very changeable. External factors such as temperature may have an impact. A chameleon that is cold or under stress will have a relatively dull appearance, being darker than normal. Males brighten their colour to signal aggression to rivals.

ABOVE BOTTOM:
Shedding
The skin of this panther chameleon is being shed, with the new skin evident beneath. When shedding, their colouration may be duller than normal. Unlike snakes, which typically shed their skin in its entirety as one piece, lizards generally lose their skin in fragments.

ABOVE TOP:
Eating habits
Having caught its food, this Oustalet's chameleon (*Furcifer oustaleti*) from Madagascar is able to break through the tough external cuticle of the invertebrate by using the sharp, v-shaped teeth that can be seen here in its mouth. Some chameleons choose to eat bees and wasps.

ABOVE BOTTOM:
A useful counterbalance
The prehensile tail of chameleons can act like another hand, helping the lizard to grasp on to a branch as it clambers around off the ground, preventing a potentially fatal fall. The tail can also serve to steady the lizard when it is targeting prey.

RIGHT:
Striking fast
A panther chameleon catches an insect. The strike is so fast that the detail is not visible to the human eye. The tip of the tongue is sticky, which helps to anchor the target so that it can be drawn back almost instantly into the mouth.

Different forms
There are various localized colour variants of the panther chameleon in northern and northeastern Madagascar where the species occurs. Some are predominantly blue, whereas others are reddish, such as the Ambilobe form. This species can also be found on offshore islets, such as Nosy Be.

ABOVE TOP:

An unusual position

Sharp spines on the body segments of the armadillo girdled lizard deter would-be predators. Its body is very flexible, so it can roll up into a ball, positioning the tip of its tail in the mouth, which gives it even better protection if threatened.

ABOVE BOTTOM AND RIGHT:

How these lizards live

An armadillo girdled lizard (*Ouroborus cataphractus*). This unusual species is found in desert areas along the western coast of South Africa. These lizards live in groups of 30 or more and will hide away in rock crevices, emerging to catch invertebrates. Females have live young.

Rivals and challenges

A common agama (*Agama agama*) sunbathing on rocks. This is a male, as reflected by its colourful appearance, with females being brownish. These lizards are highly territorial, with males challenging rivals. They live in association with up to half a dozen females and young males.

Scaled-down crocodiles
Dwarf crocodiles (*Osteolaemus species*) are the smallest true members of the crocodile clan alive today. Recent research suggests there may be two forms rather than a single species. The Congo dwarf crocodile (*O. osborni*) is the smaller, growing to just 1.2m (3.9ft).

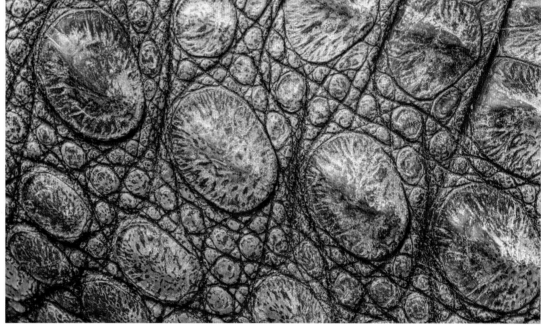

LEFT:
Range
African dwarf crocodiles are now confined to western and central parts of Africa south of the Sahara. Their range used to extend to Uganda, but they have not been recorded there since the 1940s. They favour secluded areas and are not found in large rivers.

ABOVE TOP:
Feeding habits
Fish feature prominently in the diet of the African dwarf crocodile, particularly during the wet season. When conditions are drier, they are more likely to hunt for crabs and snails. They have been known to feed on small mammals too, such as bats and shrews.

ABOVE BOTTOM:
Small size – more protection
These small crocodiles are sometimes called bony crocodiles because they are well-protected from attack by the presence of bony outgrowths called osteoderms. These extend around the neck and are also present on the underside of the body rather than running just down the back.

A lizard from southern Africa
A giant plated lizard
(*Matobosaurus validus*) with an
invertebrate that it has just caught
in its powerful jaws. It is so-called
because of the scales resembling
plates that run along its back.
These large lizards can grow to
75cm (29.5in) in length.

OPPOSITE:
Nile crocodile habitat
A typical Nile crocodile habitat is seen here in Egypt. This species often occurs in rivers and can even be encountered in brackish water but rarely ventures into the sea. It is the largest aquatic predator found in Africa, where it can be encountered in 26 different countries.

LEFT TOP:
Deadly dentition
A Nile crocodile (*Crocodylus niloticus*) has a mouth packed with as many as 68 teeth, as befits an apex predator. If they become damaged or broken, the teeth will be replaced. They all have a similar cone shape, although some teeth are bigger than others.

LEFT BOTTOM:
Social – up to a point!
Groups of Nile crocodiles can often be seen out of the water sunbathing together. However, only individuals measuring about 2m (6.6ft) and above join these groups. Smaller crocodiles face the risk of cannibalism, which is a common cause of death.

Designed for grasping
The function of the teeth of a Nile crocodile is simply to grab and hold prey effectively, preventing any escape until it can be drowned or otherwise overpowered. This is why they are all sharp and pointed. A crocodile's teeth are not used for chewing.

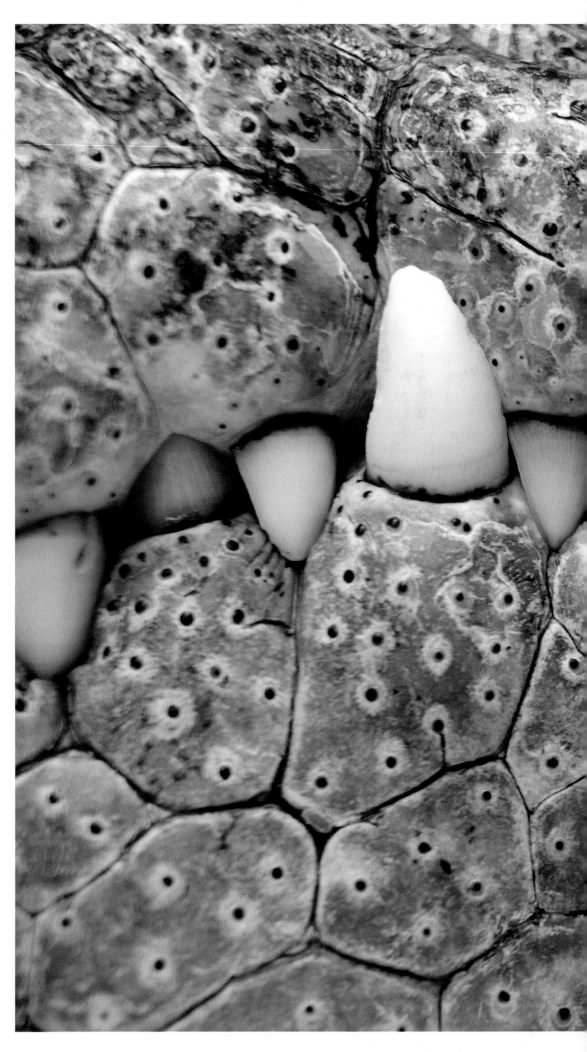

LEFT:

The gender of the hatchlings

Young Nile crocodiles hatching. The incubation temperature within the nest rather than genetics will have determined their gender. This phenomenon is called temperature-dependent sex determination (TSD). Males will ultimately grow much bigger than females, potentially reaching about 6.5m (21ft) in length.

ABOVE:

Dangerous early days

Young Nile crocodiles will call from their eggs when they are ready to hatch. Then the mother carries them to the water as shown, watching over them there at first. Nevertheless, life is perilous; on average, just one youngster in 100 survives through to adulthood.

OPPOSITE:
Feeding habits
Snails are important in the diet of adult savannah monitors. The jaws of these lizards are hinged to close with maximum force, while their flat-top teeth are ideal for cracking the shells. They will also scavenge and eat any eggs that they can find.

ABOVE:
Range and size
The savannah monitor (*Varanus exanthematicus*) is a large lizard, growing up to 1m (3.3ft) in length. It occurs in relatively arid areas of Africa south of the Sahara, extending from Senegal across to Sudan and southwards to the Democratic Republic of the Congo.

LEFT:
Lifestyle and anatomy
Young savannah monitors are more inclined to climb than adults, but this is primarily a terrestrial lizard. Their powerful forelegs are equipped with sharp claws that can be used for digging. Their strong jaws are equipped with teeth, and they also have a powerful tail.

Skin matters

The colouration of these monitor lizards varies depending on their location and age. Young hatchlings are more colourful, particularly on the sides of the body, with adults being greyer overall. Savannah monitors are common but are hunted for their skins, which are made into leather.

A striking lizard
The colourful African fire skink (*Mochlus fernandi*) grows up to 37cm (15in) and inhabits tropical forests in both West and Central Africa. It feeds mainly on invertebrate prey. Females lay clutches of 5–9 eggs, which take between 40–50 days to hatch.

ABOVE TOP:
A striped appearance
The African striped skink (*Trachylepis striata*) is common in eastern and southern parts of the continent. It has a distinctive striped appearance and typically measures 25cm (10in) in length depending on whether or not it has a complete tail. If lost, its tail can regrow.

ABOVE BOTTOM:
Staying alive
Skinks are very agile and can move quickly, either to escape predators or seize prey themselves. They have a defence mechanism shared with a number of other lizards, allowing them to lose their tail without suffering a fatal haemorrhage, thereby eluding a would-be predator.

OPPOSITE:
A distinct hierarchy
A male southern rock agama (*Agama atra*) displays its agile climbing skills here in South Africa. The species is widely distributed across southern parts of the continent. The dominant and more colourful male occupies the highest points on the rocks where a group is present.

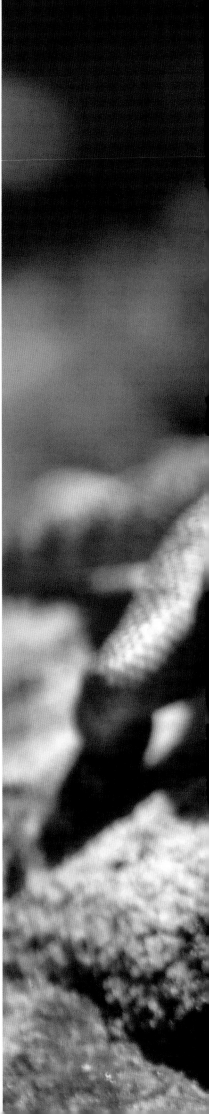

ABOVE:

Looking to stay safe

A female southern rock agama keeps a wary eye out for would-be predators, with these lizards being especially vulnerable to passing birds of prey. If alarmed, the lizards scatter and seek to retreat into crevices in the rocks until the threat has passed.

RIGHT:

Feeding habits

These rock agamas are insectivorous in their feeding habits and are able to grab crickets, locusts and other fast moving insect prey, often from relatively inaccessible locations. They occur in gardens in some areas, but here, they are particularly vulnerable to falling victim to cats.

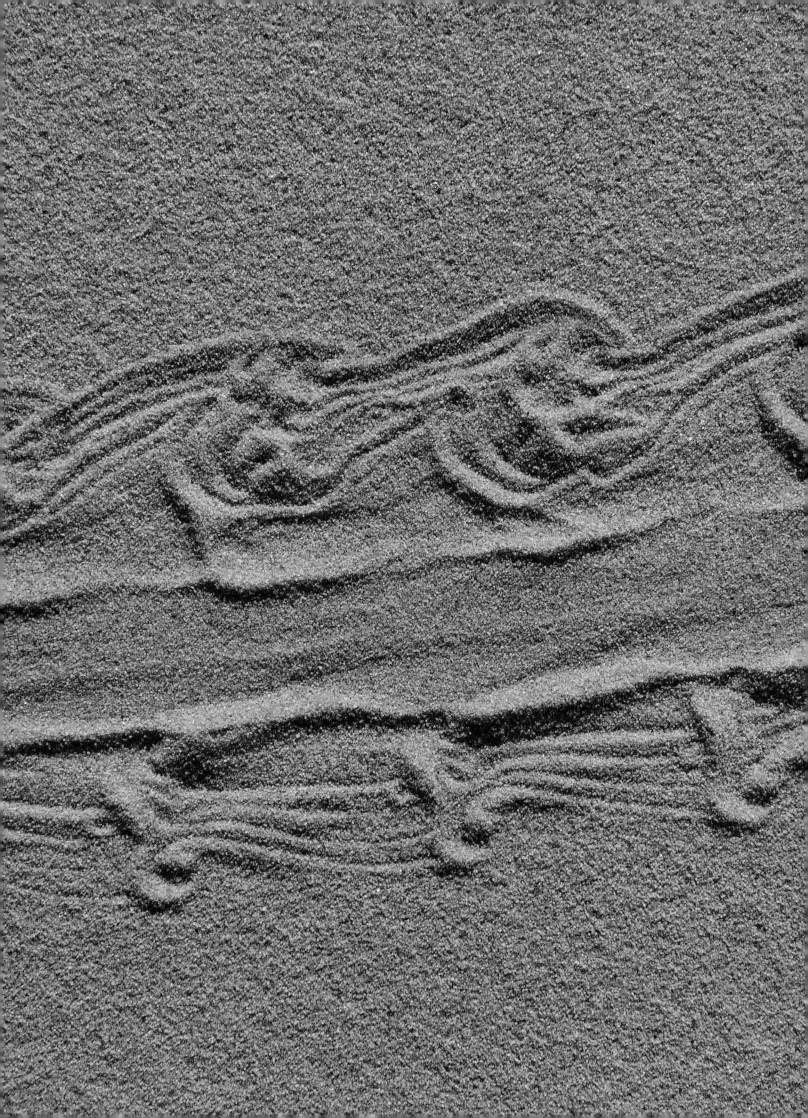

LEFT:
On the trail
Lizards may sometimes leave distinctive tracks when moving, as here in the Sahara. This is the fresh track of a North African spiny-tailed lizard (*Uromastyx acanthinura*), as can be identified by its heavy spiky tail, which it will use to protect itself if threatened.

ABOVE TOP:
Different food preferences
Uromastyx tend to differ significantly from most other lizards because they are largely herbivorous in their feeding habits. This is unusual in the case of these reptiles, with the vast majority being insectivorous and occasionally carnivorous. Even so, young uromastyx may prey on insects occasionally.

ABOVE BOTTOM:
Tail storage
The East African spiny-tailed lizard (*Cordylus tropidosternum*) occurs in dry forested areas. It lacks the heavy tail of uromastyx lizards, using this part of its body as a fat store to help it survive the dry season when the availability of invertebrates is scarce.

Well-protected
A Moroccan spiny-tailed lizard (*Uromastyx nigriventris*). These lizards, occurring in Morocco and western Algeria, are active during the day, retreating to underground burrows when the sun is at its hottest. Their colouration provides camouflage, and their manoeuvrable, spiked tail can be seen clearly here.

ABOVE TOP:

A wide distribution

The range of the Sudan plated lizard (*Broadleysaurus major*) extends much more widely than just Sudan. It occurs in the eastern parts of the continent right down to South Africa and is present on the island of Zanzibar. It also ranges across central parts to Ghana.

ABOVE BOTTOM:

Good protection

Also known as the giant plated lizard, this species can grow relatively large – up to 60cm (24in) in the case of the males, which reach a bigger size overall than females. These colourful lizards are well-protected by their distinctive plate-like scales.

RIGHT:

Open country

Sudan plated lizards prefer areas of savannah, which serve to provide some tree cover. They particularly favour locations where there are rocky outcrops, which act as retreats if danger threatens. They can also be encountered in coastal regions but are not found in dense forest anywhere.

Highly endangered
A West African slender-snouted crocodile (*Mecistops cataphractus*) emerges from its egg. This species is one of the most critically endangered crocodilians in the world, with a population estimated to be comprised of just 500 individuals. It lives in very remote, inaccessible areas of habitat.

Lifestyle

The narrow jaws of the West African slender-snouted crocodile help it to seize fish, which make up a significant part of its diet. The crocodilians can grow up to a length of about 4.5m (15ft) in the case of the biggest males.

Asia

The Asian continent is home to about 3500 species of reptile, and among these are both the biggest crocodile and the largest lizard in the world. The saltwater crocodile (*Crocodylus porosus*) is a giant that actually spans continents thanks to its seagoing habits. It is the nearest species alive today to the marine crocodiles known from the fossil record and can be found in coastal areas from India southwards, as well as being widely distributed throughout the Philippines and Indonesia, extending southwards from New Guinea across the Torres Strait to northern Australia.

In contrast, the Komodo dragon (*Varanus komodoensis*) only occurs on four small Indonesian islands – Komodo, Rinca, Flores and Gili Motang – which make up part of the Lesser Sundas group.

Other large monitors occur in Asia, and some share the Komodo dragon's swimming abilities, but none are as large. There is also a wide range of other lizards – especially members of the agamid group – that occur on the continent, particularly in areas of tropical rainforest.

A distinctive range of Asian crocodilians can be encountered there too, including the distinctive gharial (*Gavialis gangeticus*) plus the only member of the alligator family to be found outside of the Americas in the guise of the Chinese alligator (*Alligator sinensis*). More generalist crocodiles with a localized range can be encountered on various islands such as New Guinea, but undoubtedly, it is the saltwater crocodile that poses the greatest danger to people.

OPPOSITE:
Battling together
Two Asian water monitors (*Varanus salvator*) battle each other for supremacy. This particular monitor is very widely encountered in southern and southeastern parts of the continent. As their name suggests, they can swim well and may plunge into water to escape if under threat.

A powerful swimmer
An Asian water monitor climbs up a tree. Note the narrow ridge running down the top of the tail, which helps these semi-aquatic lizards to swim well, with the tail serving rather like a rudder. They propel themselves by using their strong limbs too.

RIGHT TOP:

Feeding habits

Fish may feature prominently in the diet of Asian water monitors, along with other aquatic prey, such as crabs, frogs and turtles, but they will also hunt mammals and birds.

RIGHT BOTTOM:

Heavily traded

Although common in Asia, these lizards are killed in huge numbers each year for their skins, which are used to supply the leather trade, being made into items like belts.

OPPOSITE:

Size matters

A young Asian water monitor. These lizards are much more colourful at this stage. Ultimately, they can grow to 3.2m (10.5ft) long and weigh 50kg (110lb).

A limited range
The Chinese alligator used to be found over a much wider area, even being present in Japan, but today, it is confined to just a small area of China, mainly in Anhui province in the far east of the country. Unfortunately, it is critically endangered.

OVERLEAF:
A small size
These alligators hatch from the smallest eggs laid by any crocodilian and typically measure 20cm (8in) on hatching. They only attain a length of about 2.1m (7ft), weighing up to 45kg (100lb). Snails feature prominently in their diet.

A seasonal lifestyle
Living in a region where the
temperature becomes cold in
winter, the Chinese alligator will
brumate (become dormant) from
the end of October to mid-April,
retreating to burrows that it digs.
These can be complex structures
up to 25m (82ft) long.

ABOVE:
A striking appearance
Chinese water dragons (*Physignathus cocincinus*) are large lizards that can grow up to 90cm (3ft) in length, although most of their length is accounted for by their long tail. Males are bigger in size than females and also tend to be more colourful.

OPPOSITE:
Lifestyle
These lizards are found in tropical forest, often close to water, where the temperature is hot and relatively constant through the year. They are active during the day, feeding on a very varied diet, including fruit, invertebrates and even birds' eggs, and may occasionally swim.

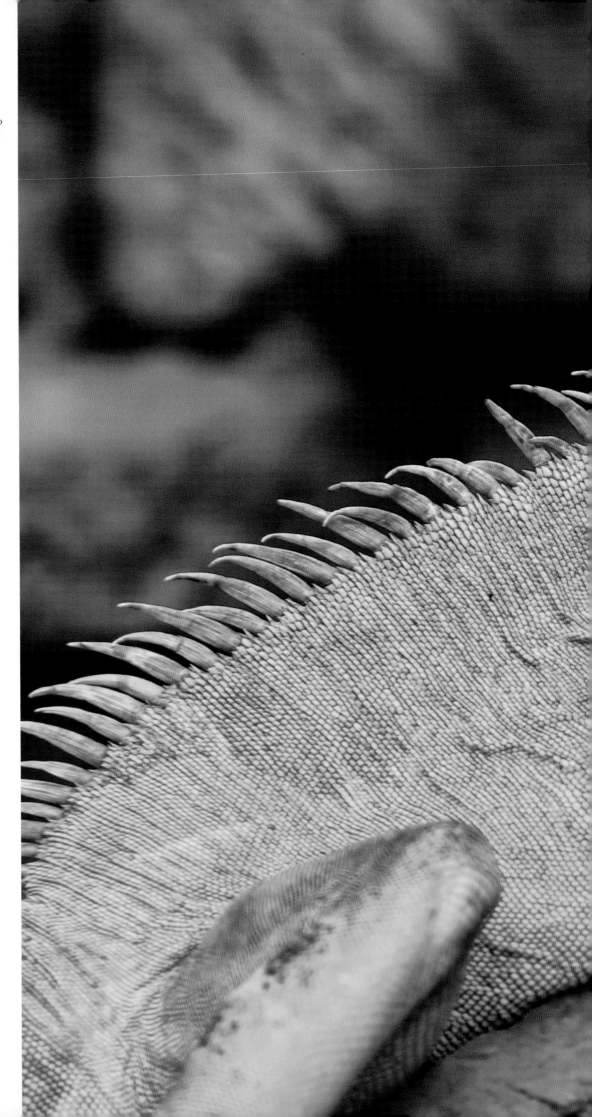

An amazing ability
The range of the Chinese water dragon extends across a wider area of southeastern Asia and is actually not confined exclusively to China. If frightened, an individual may jump off a branch into water and can remain submerged there for up to 90 minutes.

LEFT:

On the brink

A view inside the narrow, tooth-filled jaws of the gharial, a predominantly fish-eating crocodilian. It used to have a wide distribution in the major river systems of the northern Indian subcontinent but is now critically endangered because of hunting, habitat change and pollution.

ABOVE TOP:

Trying to assist

Reintroduction programmes are now being employed in an attempt to boost the numbers of this unique crocodilian, which presents no danger to people in spite of its large size. This, in the case of the larger males, can be up to 6m (19.7ft).

ABOVE BOTTOM:

Changing challenges

Although shooting of gharials for their skins and as trophies started their decline, changing the course of rivers, creating dams and mining along river banks, reducing the areas available for nesting, are much more significant factors today. These crocodilians can also drown in fishing nets.

PREVIOUS PAGE:

Hope for the future

Gharials are now being captive-bred. Females lay up to 60 eggs in a clutch, with their eggs being the largest of any living crocodilian. Gharials are highly aquatic and struggle to walk on land. They feed underwater, having about 110 teeth in their mouth.

LEFT:

An amazing discovery

The Komodo dragon remained unknown to science up until 1910. When it was first reported, its huge size suggested that it was probably a land crocodile rather than a lizard. These giants can grow to 3m (9.8ft) and are capable of killing people.

ABOVE TOP AND BOTTOM:
Changing lifestyle
As adults, Komodo dragons can weigh up to 70kg (150lb) and are no longer able to climb easily, although youngsters will spend time off the ground, where they cannot fall prey to large individuals. Their claws are powerful and can inflict serious injuries.

RIGHT:
Food-finding ability
The distinctive forked tongue of the Komodo dragon helps these lizards to find food, picking up scent molecules in the air, which then register on the vomeronasal organ in the roof of the mouth. They can detect carrion up to 9.5km (6 miles) away.

ABOVE:
Prey
Komodo dragons possess a pair of venom glands in their lower jaw aside from a formidable array of some 60 teeth. They will attack large prey, such as wild pigs or cattle, and can usually simply overpower their quarry rather than relying on their venom.

RIGHT:
Komodo battle
Two Komodo dragons rearing up on their hind legs battle with each other. It has recently been found that although they may suffer serious injuries when fighting, these giant lizards have an unusual compound in their blood which guards against infection and promotes wound healing.

An unusual lizard
The leopard gecko (*Eublepharis macularius*) is a small lizard found in dry grassland and desert areas, from eastern Iran via Pakistan to northern India to Nepal. It is an atypical gecko because it lacks the expanded toe pads that allow geckos to climb vertical surfaces.

Skilled hunters

Insectivorous by nature, leopard geckos are opportunistic hunters, taking whatever prey is within reach and being able to move fast over the ground when required. They have become very popular pets and now also occur in a range of selectively bred colours, as in this case.

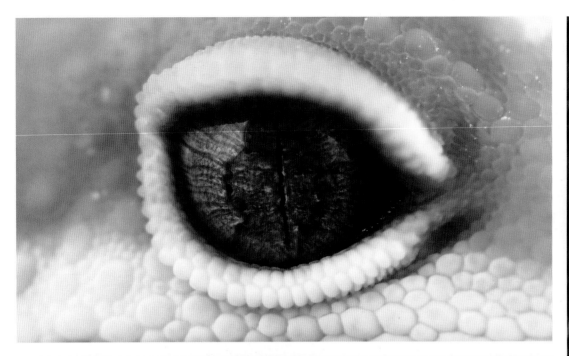

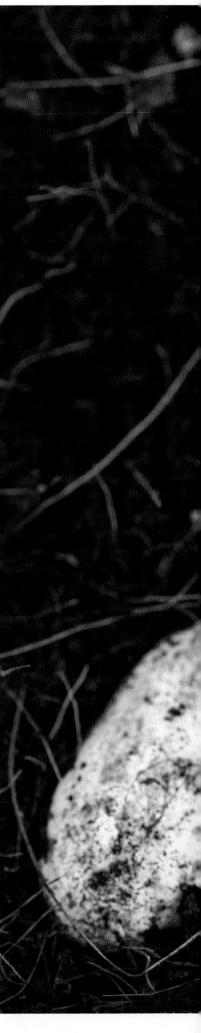

ABOVE TOP:
Revealing eyes
The eye of the leopard gecko gives a clue as to its lifestyle. The slit-shaped pupils reveal this is primarily a nocturnal species that hides away during the daytime, only emerging to hunt as dusk falls. It can see well under these darker conditions.

ABOVE BOTTOM:
A new skin
A leopard gecko sheds its skin. The imprint of the scales is mirrored here. Shedding allows the lizard to grow, and initially, it may appear more brightly coloured. The markings on the head, for example, will nevertheless remain unaltered after the shedding process is complete.

RIGHT:
Changing appearances
A young leopard gecko hatchling emerges from its egg. These lizards are unusual because at this early age, they display a banded patterning. However, this is lost in adulthood and replaced by the characteristic spotted patterning that accounts for the common name of these geckos.

Range

The false gharial (*Tomistoma schlegelii*) is a crocodilian which is present on the islands of Borneo, Sumatra and possibly Java. On the Asian mainland, it is now restricted to Peninsular Malaysia, although it used to be found over a wider area, including Thailand and Vietnam.

ABOVE TOP:
A large size
The skull of the false gharial is longer than that of any other living crocodilian, measuring up to 84cm (33in), with a narrow snout that can be 104cm (41in) long. Such giants may have reached nearly 6.1m (20ft) overall.

ABOVE BOTTOM:
Declining habitat
These crocodilians are rarely found in rivers today, with the species now being found largely in inaccessible and more remote swampy areas. Drainage projects and forest clearance represent significant threats to the survival of this species. Their eggs are also sought after locally as food.

RIGHT:
A versatile predator
Given their narrow snouts, false gharials were thought to eat only fish, but it is now clear that they take a much more varied diet, including monkeys, deer, birds and other reptiles. There have even been several fatal attacks on people recorded over recent years.

RIGHT:
Nesting habits
Female false gharials make a nest mound where they bury their eggs. Their clutch size is unlikely to exceed 35 eggs in total, but they are the largest eggs laid by any species of crocodilian.

OPPOSITE TOP:
A hazardous early life
A young false gharial, recognizable by its more colourful appearance compared to an adult. A key difference in the breeding habits of this species is that after laying, the female abandons the nest.

BELOW:
Worrying times
Conservation measures are underway, but a study in Sumatra has shown their range there has been reduced by up to 40 per cent because of development over the past 75 years, and the evidence suggests a growing risk of conflict with people.

ABOVE TOP:
Distribution
A mugger crocodile (*Crocodylus palustris*) rests alongside the Chambai River in India's northern state of Uttar Pradesh. The range of this species extends across the Indian subcontinent from southern Iran, and it also occurs on the island of Sri Lanka, being protected throughout its range.

ABOVE BOTTOM:
Lifestyle
These crocodiles occur in a variety of different habitats, from rivers and lakes to marshes, explaining their alternative name of marsh crocodile. It is not a particularly large species, attaining a maximum size of about 5m (16.4ft), and it is confined to freshwater areas.

RIGHT:
Threats to survival
In spite of being protected, mugger crocodiles do suffer from habitat destruction, such as drainage of marshland areas. Some are also killed annually in both road and rail collisions, and smaller individuals in particular may become entangled in fishing nets and drown as a result.

A hungry crocodile
Fish feature prominently in the diet of mugger crocodiles. But they have also been observed using sticks held in their jaws as perches in order to attract birds, which can then be caught. This is the first case of actual tool use documented in reptiles.

On the move
During the dry season, mugger crocodiles can be forced to move over land in search of more suitable habitat. With fewer places to drink, mammals and birds may then feature more prominently as prey at this stage, while the crocodiles lurk hidden in waterholes.

Range divider
A New Guinea crocodile (*Crocodylus novaeguineae*). This small species is found north of the mountain range that divides the island. It is now considered to be a separate species from Hall's New Guinea crocodile (*Crocodylus halli*), which occurs to the south of this geographical barrier.

OPPOSITE:
Seeing in the dark
In relative darkness, the pupil in each eye opens automatically, allowing more light through to the retina where the image forms. A reflective layer behind that called the tapetum lucidum explains why the crocodilian's eyes glow if a light is shone on them after dark.

ABOVE:
A shy nature
New Guinea crocodiles live in slow-flowing water where aquatic vegetation is often plentiful. They lurk largely hidden during the day with their nose and eyes just above the surface.

LEFT:
Underwater vision
Crocodiles have a keen sense of vision, enabling them to detect danger or potential prey. They have a thin, transparent membrane covering the eyes and so can see underwater too.

An underwater view
Here each eye is protected by a nictitating membrane, and the crocodile keeps its legs more parallel with its body than on land, becoming streamlined, which means it can swim faster. The muscular tail provides propulsive power and allows the crocodile to steer its course.

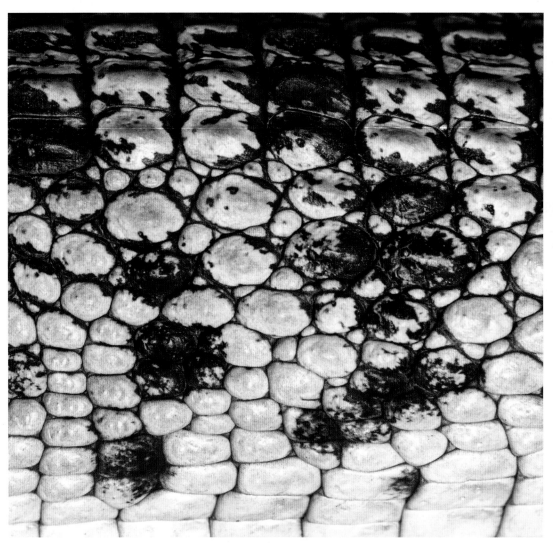

ABOVE:
Body protection
A close-up of the skin of a Philippine crocodile (*Crocodylus mindorensis*). This species has a series of heavy protective shields running down its back. Its colour darkens with age.

OPPOSITE TOP:
Status
The Philippine crocodile is found only in the Philippines, where it is very scarce, having already become extinct on some islands. It is regarded as the rarest crocodile alive today.

RIGHT:
Island issues
These are small freshwater crocodiles, with the larger males only growing up to a maximum length of approximately 3.5m (11ft). Their dependence on freshwater means that populations are isolated, and a fall in numbers can have a significant impact on their genetic diversity.

Mistaken identity
In spite of its relatively small size, many people in the Philippines are fearful of this endemic species, although it poses little risk unless challenged, with its diet being comprised largely of fish. Confusion with much more dangerous saltwater crocodiles is undoubtedly an issue.

LEFT:

A true giant

The saltwater crocodile ranks as the biggest reptile alive today. Large males can reach lengths of at least 6.3m (21ft), weighing in at a gigantic 1500kg (3300lb). Females, in comparison, are much smaller, reaching just 3m (10ft) overall.

ABOVE TOP:

Adaptable by nature

One of the unique features of these big crocodiles is that they can swim long distances at sea, possessing special glands near their eyes that enable them to excrete excess salt from their bodies. They can move from freshwater rivers into estuaries and coastal areas.

ABOVE BOTTOM:

A varied diet

Saltwater crocodiles are highly adaptable in their feeding habits, being opportunistic hunters. They will even tackle fearsome bull sharks in coastal waters and are able to crush the shells of adult sea turtles in their jaws. Even tigers have occasionally fallen victim to these crocodiles.

Incredible strength

The saltwater crocodile has the more powerful bite of any living animal, as reflected by the bulging musculature on each side of the head. They can also leap almost vertically from the water, with sufficient force to knock down prey located on a branch above.

Deadly attacks

Larger male saltwater crocodiles are particularly dangerous to people. In some cases, however, fatal attacks may not be triggered by their desire to hunt, but rather because small boats powered by outboard motors can be confused with another crocodile entering into an established male's territory.

Siamese crocodile
A Siamese crocodile (*Crocodylus siamensis*) photographed basking in the wild in Thailand, which was previously known as Siam, thereby explaining the name of this species. These crocodiles can also be encountered more widely in southeast Asia, south to Indonesia, although they are no longer numerous.

ABOVE:
Widespread farming
Although these crocodiles are now exceedingly rare in the wild, there are an estimated 700,000 of them on commercial crocodile farms in the region, being kept primarily for their skins.

RIGHT:
Its importance
The skin of Siamese crocodiles, as with many crocodilians, is very valuable in the leather trade, and farming has helped to provide local people with an important source of revenue.

OPPOSITE:
Different challenges
It is ironic that Siamese crocodiles rank as one of the most critically endangered crocodiles in the wild, but this is not just the result of hunting pressure. Unfortunately, habitat loss is a major issue when it comes to conserving them in their natural habitat.

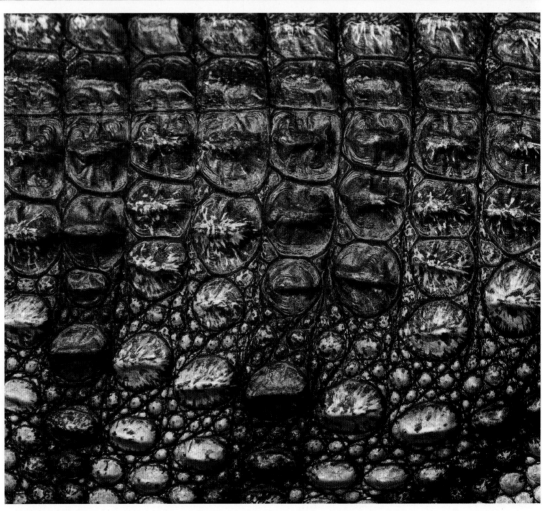

Hybridization

Simply using farmed Siamese crocodiles and reintroducing them to the wild is not straightforward either, partly because many have been hybridized with saltwater crocodiles, as their offspring grow to a larger size. A true Siamese crocodile will only reach about 3m (9.8ft) long.

LEFT:

Well-equipped to hunt

A tokay gecko (*Gekko gecko*) seen with its mouth open, revealing the formidable array of small but sharp teeth in the jaws of this lizard. It is probably the third largest gecko alive today, typically growing to a length of about 30cm (12in).

ABOVE TOP:

An unusual name

The long tongue of this species allows it to wipe the surface of its eyes. Its unusual name 'tokay' derives from the sound of its calls. These geckos occur over a wide area of the continent, from India eastwards through southeast Asia down to Indonesia.

ABOVE BOTTOM:

Nighttime predators

Tokay geckos are nocturnal hunters capable of tackling large invertebrates and even small vertebrates, such as newly hatched birds. Like many geckos, they have adapted well to human dwellings, moving into homes where nighttime flying insects are often attracted by lights, meaning that prey is plentiful for them.

ALL PHOTOGRAPHS:
Gecko scales
The bluish and orange scales of tokay geckos varies between individuals, and they are also able to adjust their appearance somewhat, darkening their body colour for example. They can climb well, aided by foot pads that allow them to scale vertical surfaces without any difficulty.

An aggressive demeanour
Tokay geckos tend to display strong territorial instincts, with the larger males being aggressive by nature. Unfortunately, the numbers of this impressive lizard have declined significantly over recent years as they have been sought after by the oriental medicine trade for a variety of purposes.

Australias and the Pacific

Australia is home to a large number of lizards but only two species of crocodilian. One of these (also featured in the Asian section) is the fearsome seagoing saltwater crocodile. There are still large monitor lizards to be found in Australia, but those alive today would have been dwarfed by megalania (*Varanus priscus*), which stalked the continent during the Pleistocene epoch. It died out about 50,000 years ago but not before encountering the first human settlers of the continent. Whether they may have played a part in the extinction of this apex predator, however, is unclear. Megalania is the biggest lizard yet discovered, and it is thought to have grown up to 7m (23ft) in length and to have weighed as much as 1940kg (4277lb). There was also a large terrestrial crocodile, known as quinkana, which is believed to have reached a size of up to 7m (23ft) in length. Its long legs were located directly under its body rather than to the side. Another point of distinction compared with contemporary aquatic crocodilians is the fact that its teeth could sheer through flesh rather than simply being sharp and serving to grip on to prey. Out on the Pacific islands, lizards are relatively commonplace, having proved to be capable of reaching these often isolated locations, but the only crocodilian that may be encountered in the region is – yet again – the saltwater crocodile.

OPPOSITE:
Widely kept
The bearded dragon (*Pogona vitticeps*) is an Australian species of agamid lizard that is probably the most popular pet lizard in the world. 'Beardies' are known to be able to identity their keeper by sight. This is one of the numerous colour variants that now exist.

ABOVE TOP:
Colour changes
Bearded dragons, which originate in the central region of the Australian continent, are able to vary their colouration to a limited extent, like many lizards, depending partly on environmental factors, such as temperature. When cold, they turn darker, allowing them to absorb heat more quickly.

ABOVE BOTTOM:
The importance of their claws
Bearded dragons have strong claws, which enable them to dig when required. A female will excavate a nest site for her eggs, for example. These lizards also use their claws to climb, frequently preferring to bask off the ground, particularly when they are young.

RIGHT:
Explaining their name
Bearded dragons are territorial, and if an individual feels threatened, it will react by not just puffing up its body in a bid to appear larger but also by inflating the spiky beard under its chin.

A smallish crocodilian
The freshwater crocodile
(*Crocodylus johnsoni*) is confined
to northern-central parts of
Australia, living exclusively in
areas of freshwater as its name
suggests. It is characterized by a
relatively narrow snout and small
size, with the larger males growing
up to 2.1m (6.9ft).

OVERLEAF:
An introduced killer
The number of freshwater
crocodiles has plummeted over
recent years, primarily because
of the introduction of the cane
toad (*Rhinella marina*), which
has spread across Australia. The
crocodiles seek to eat the toads or
their tadpoles and are poisoned by
the toxin they release.

LEFT:

Loss and rediscovery

The crested gecko (*Correlophus ciliatus*) first became known to science in 1866, but then, some time later, it was feared to be extinct before being rediscovered in 1994. It occurs on South Province on the island of New Caledonia, lying to the east of Australia.

ABOVE TOP:

Lifestyle

These geckos are very agile and can climb well, being arboreal by nature, living in the canopy of the rainforest. Like many lizards, they can lose their tail as a defence against predators, but in this particular case, the tail is not regrown once lost.

ABOVE BOTTOM:

A surprising threat

The future of these geckos seems relatively secure, although introduced little fire ants (*Wassmania auropunctata*) will prey on them, overwhelming individuals with their combined stinging power. The ants also take invertebrates that crested geckos would eat. An ever-present risk from wildfires poses another danger.

ALL PHOTOGRAPHS:
Crested gecko
The crested gecko is also known as the eyelash gecko thanks to the hair-like projections around its eyes, and it is nocturnal, as the slit-like shape of its pupils reveals. In addition to invertebrates, this species also feeds on ripe fruit and nectar.

LEFT:
The purpose of the frill
The frilled lizard (*Chlamydosaurus kingii*) reveals its spectacular frill created by a flap of skin that extends right around the neck and can be raised in this way by the lizard if it feels under threat or as part of its courtship. Both sexes have frills.

OVERLEAF LEFT TOP:
Lifestyle
A close-up study of the toe of a frilled lizard, which terminates in a sharp claw. Their claws assist in climbing, digging and probably removing invertebrates out of tree bark or other inaccessible places, with these lizards being largely insectivorous in their feeding habits.

OVERLEAF LEFT BOTTOM:
Frill design
Here, the frill is folded down alongside the lizard's head, having a ridged appearance. These lizards vary quite widely in colouration, not just in terms of their body colouration but also their frills. These can range from red and orange shades through to yellow and white.

OVERLEAF RIGHT:
Size
Frilled lizards have a relatively long, slender tail, which they can direct forward over their head, as shown here. Males are bigger than females overall and can grow to 90cm (35in) in total length. They are territorial and often fight rivals during the breeding season.

Saltwater crocodile
A saltwater crocodile in close-up, showing its powerful teeth, claws and tail. This species is Australia's apex predator, and protection measures over recent decades have paid off. In the Northern Territory alone, the population has soared from just 3000 during the 1970s to 100,000 today.

LEFT:
Diet
There has been a change in the diet of saltwater crocodiles in Australia since their numbers started to recover, as they have started preying far more on land mammals, according to research. The crocodiles are now hunting large mammals, notably feral pigs, buffaloes and wallabies.

OVERLEAF:
Nests
Although no wild predators will challenge a fully grown saltwater crocodile, their nests may be raided by goanna lizards and buffalos can trample the site, destroying the eggs. Nevertheless, female crocodiles can lay 50 eggs per clutch, which helps to explain the species' dramatic recovery.

ABOVE:
New habitats
As it stands, it appears that these crocodiles may be expanding their range in Australia, swimming out to sea and then travelling along the coastline, looking for new riverine habitats.

RIGHT:
Growing up
Young saltwater crocodiles measure just under 30cm (12in) when they hatch, and it will be over a decade before they are ready to breed for the first time.

OPPOSITE BOTTOM:
Prey
When the young hatch, they are at risk of falling prey to other, bigger crocodiles as well as barramundi, which are predatory fish, plus turtles and possibly large wading birds.

Thorny devil
This strange-looking lizard
is known as the thorny devil
(*Moloch horridus*). It occurs
over much of the western half of
Australia, notably in the central
parts. It can grow to 21cm (8.3in),
with females in this case being
slightly larger than males.

ABOVE TOP:

Camouflage

The bizarre appearance of these agamid lizards is thought to provide them with camouflage, confusing would-be predators. The scales making up their spiky appearance act less obviously as channels, helping these lizards direct any rainwater falling in this arid landscape to their mouths.

ABOVE BOTTOM AND RIGHT:

Hidden in plain sight

The thorny devil pauses every few moments when moving, rocking back and forth on its legs. From a distance away, this performance might help the lizard to appear like a piece of dry vegetation being blown on a breeze, effectively disguising it in plain sight.

Confusion reigns

A predator encountering the thorny devil may be confused about where to strike because it has an evident swollen area at the back of the head. If confronted, the lizard lowers its real head, encouraging a strike at this false target made of soft tissue.

Europe

The number of reptiles to be found in Europe is significantly lower than on any other continent, with only about 280 in total being found in this region. There are no crocodilians, although they used to occur there in the past, as evidenced by the fossil record. The lizards that are present are generally quite small in size. The largest group is made up of the so-called wall lizards, which belong to the family Lacertidae. There are few agamid lizards, but geckos are nevertheless quite common, being found predominantly in warmer Mediterranean areas. Some species which have been inadvertently introduced here, being brought in with goods from elsewhere, are now established. There is also a native European chameleon (*Chamaeleo chameleon*), which has a lifestyle not dissimilar to that of its far more numerous African relatives. Slowworms (*Anguis* species), which at first glance could be confused with a snake, are another of the more distinctive lizards represented in Europe. They demonstrate a characteristic shared with various other European lizards in that they produce live young rather than laying eggs. This reproductive method has the advantage of ensuring that the survival of the species does not depend on the vagaries of the weather and whether the summer will be hot enough for the lizard's eggs to hatch successfully. On the downside, however, with a growing brood inside her, the female and her offspring are exposed to great risk of predation prior to birth.

OPPOSITE:
Wide-ranging
A sand lizard (*Lacerta agilis*). This member of the wall lizard group is one of the most widely distributed species in Europe, being found from France eastwards right across to Russia. It even occurs as far north as Scandinavia where it has a small foothold.

FAR LEFT:

Appearance

The male sand lizard can be easily distinguished, displaying green colouration rather than just shades of brown like the female. Males are also slightly larger, reaching 19.5cm (7.7in).

ABOVE TOP, BOTTOM AND LEFT:

Lifestyle

Sand lizards hunt insects, and in spite of their name, they can be found in a wide range of habitats. When breeding, females produce up to 15 eggs per clutch.

209

ABOVE:

Characteristics

A pair of European green lizards. The female here can be recognized, as she is not so vividly coloured. Young hatchlings are pale brown overall, but within the year, they will have acquired their adult colouration and can grow up to 40cm (16in).

OPPOSITE TOP:

Habitat differences

A European green lizard seen drinking water from a puddle. The distribution of this species extends basically from France southeastwards right down through Italy and reaches northern parts of Spain as well. In southern areas where it is warmer, these lizards prefer damper surroundings.

OPPOSITE BOTTOM:

Warming up

Rocks provide a natural heat reservoir, from which the European green lizard benefits by being able to absorb this heat into its body. Sunbathing also provides the opportunity to benefit from the sun's ultraviolet rays, allowing the lizard to manufacture vitamin D in its body.

OPPOSITE:
Looking around
European green lizards use their sharp claws for climbing, as seen here, although they tend to be terrestrial in their habits.

ABOVE:
A snake-like appearance
The scheltopusik (*Pseudopus apodus*), also known as the European legless lizard and the European glass lizard, ranges from southern Europe into Asia.

LEFT TOP AND BOTTOM:
A true lizard
A feature that sets scheltopusiks apart from snakes is they have eyelids and can blink. Their body has a segmented appearance.

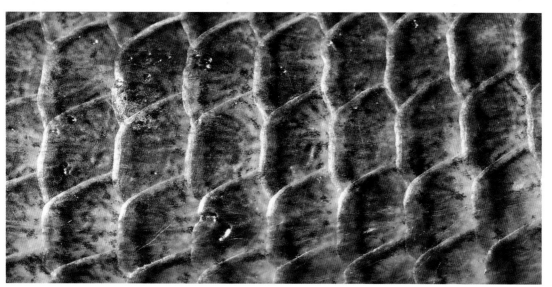

Scheltopusiks

Scheltopusiks are Europe's largest lizard, growing up to 1.35m (4.4ft) in length. Although they appear to have no legs, there may be very tiny rear legs, measuring just 2mm (0.08in), visible on the underside of the body near the cloacal opening.

LEFT:

An endemic form

A Greek rock lizard
(*Hellenolacerta graeca*). This
species has a limited distribution,
being found only in parts of
southern Greece occurring in
the Peloponnese region, either in
woodland relatively close to water
or in rocky areas up to an altitude
of 1600m (5200ft).

ABOVE TOP:

Staying safe

Like other rock lizards, this species
will take advantage of retreats that
it can use, which provide a good
vantage point. Nevertheless, if
attacked, a Greek rock lizard can
shed part of its tail, which may
allow it to escape safely in the
ensuing confusion.

ABOVE BOTTOM:

Visual distinctions

It is possible to sex these rock
lizards quite easily, with females
displaying less spotting on the
back, and any blue markings (if
present) extend along the body in
the case of males but are confined
to the vicinity of the shoulder area
in females.

Diversity in the population
A Tyrrhenian wall lizard (*Podarcis tiliguerta*) basking on a granite rock on the Italian island of Sardinia. Although only found here and on the neighbouring Mediterranean island of Corsica, there are ten distinctive forms of this lizard recognized by zoologists within its rather limited range.

LEFT:
Adaptable nature
Tyrrhenian wall lizards are very adaptable. They can be seen in a wide range of different habitats, ranging from rocky landscapes, as seen here, to forested areas and grassland, and they even venture into gardens. Like others of their kind, they hunt invertebrates of various types.

ABOVE:
A rethink
A Tyrrhenian wall lizard looks out from its hiding spot. The wide diversity in their appearance is remarkable, as is evident across both islands and associated islets, but recent research suggests the individuals here may represent more than one species of wall lizard.

ABOVE TOP:
An incredible survivor
A viviparous lizard (*Zootoca vivipara*). It has the most northerly distribution of any land-dwelling reptile, extending up into northern Norway, which lies within the Arctic Circle. Most populations are viviparous, giving birth to live young, but two southern European ones reproduce by laying eggs.

ABOVE BOTTOM:
Key distinctions
Females vary in colour, with some having a yellowish tinge, while others are more orangish, and a third group display intermediate colouration. Males can be identified by their broader head shape compared with females, and those with the biggest heads dominate in terms of mating.

RIGHT:
Staying alive
These lizards are well-equipped to survive the severe freezing winters that occur in parts of their range. They seek out areas where the soil remains relatively warm, hibernating there, and may survive being frozen over the winter period without sustaining any obvious physiological damage.

Picture Credits